Editor
Sarah Beatty

Editorial Project Manager
Mara Ellen Guckian

Editor-in-Chief
Sharon Coan, M.S. Ed.

Illustrator
Alexandra Artigas

Cover Artist
Barb Lorseyedi

Art Coordinator
Kevin Barnes

Imaging
James Edward Grace
Rosa C. See

Product Manager
Phil Garcia

Publishers
Rachelle Cracchiolo, M.S. Ed.
Mary Dupuy Smith, M.S. Ed.

Skill Builders
for
Young Learners
Math

Early Childhood

D1318439

Author

Amy DeCastro, M.A.

Teacher Created Materials

Teacher Created Materials, Inc.
6421 Industry Way
Westminster, CA 92683
www.teachercreated.com
ISBN-0-7439-3686-8
©2002 Teacher Created Materials, Inc.
Made in U.S.A.

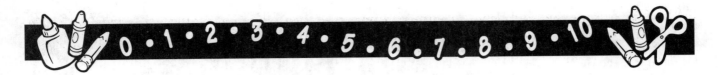

Table of Contents

Introduction

The level of skills expected to be learned by kindergartners today is profoundly different from what it was two decades ago. It is also true that most children entering kindergarten have much wider experience outside the home than children of the past. Therefore, students are expected to demonstrate basic skills knowledge at an earlier age. Fortunately, with just a pinch of encouragement, little ones are naturally curious and eager to learn.

Skill Builders for Young Learners: Math is the perfect way to reinforce math principles taught in school. It provides teachers, tutors, and parents with a multitude of math concepts that are explored in easy-to-follow pages. The skills include visual discrimination, numbers and number symbols, counting and number order, sorting and comparing, patterning, shapes, sizes, concepts of more or less, positioning, identifying sets of objects, and simple addition.

This practice book is laid out in a graduated sequence of one-page, enjoyable practice activities for young children that will promote self-confidence and an enthusiasm for learning. Crayons, pencils, glue, and scissors are the only supplies required.

This book was designed to be compatible with any early childhood curriculum. It is a tool to help awaken in children the joy of learning basic math skills and vocabulary in a low-pressure environment. The activities are great for enrichment, classroom practice, tutoring, home schooling, or just for fun.

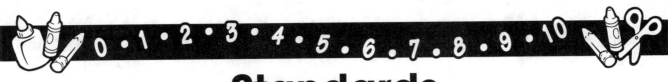

Standards

Counting—Students recite numerals in ascending order by ones to ten.

Identifying and Creating Sets of Objects—Students understand the relationship between numbers and quantities by using one-to-one correspondence.

More or Less—Students compare two or more sets of objects and identify which set is equal to, more than, or less than others.

Numbers and Number Symbols—Students understand, identify, write, compare, and represent whole numbers to ten with numerals and words.

Number Order—Students understand and identify the placement of numerals to ten.

Patterning—Students identify and reproduce a sequence with attributes.

Positioning—Students identify appropriate placement of objects in sequence.

Shapes—Students name, describe, sort, and draw two-dimensional objects.

Simple Addition—Students use objects and operations to determine answers to combined numbers.

Size—Students distinguish between the physical dimensions of objects.

Sort and Compare—Students develop spatial sense by identifying different attributes such as color, shape, size, and other properties for classifying objects.

Visual Discrimination—Students see and understand similarities and differences in objects and pictures.

0 • 1 • 2 • 3 • 4 • 5 • 6 • 7 • 8 • 9 • 10

Biggest

 Color the biggest object in each row.

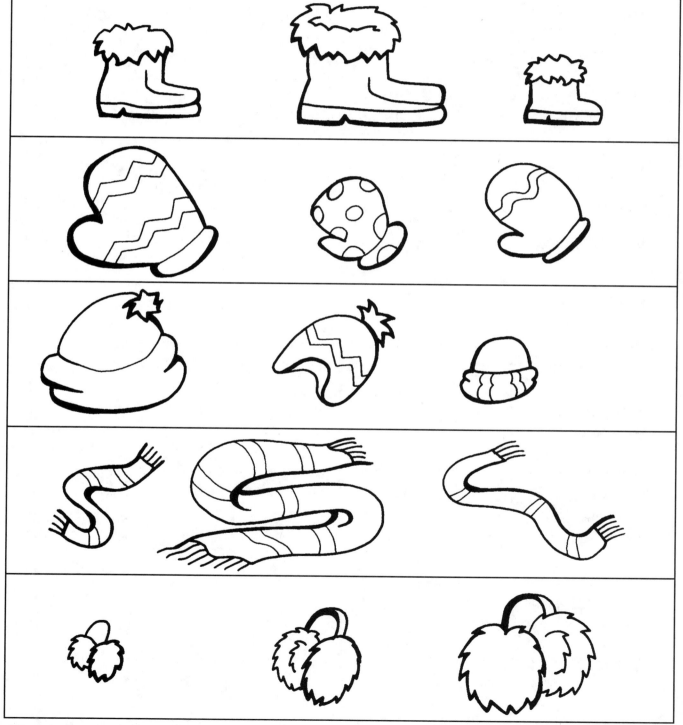

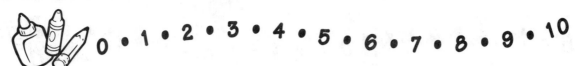

Smallest

 Color the smallest object in each row.

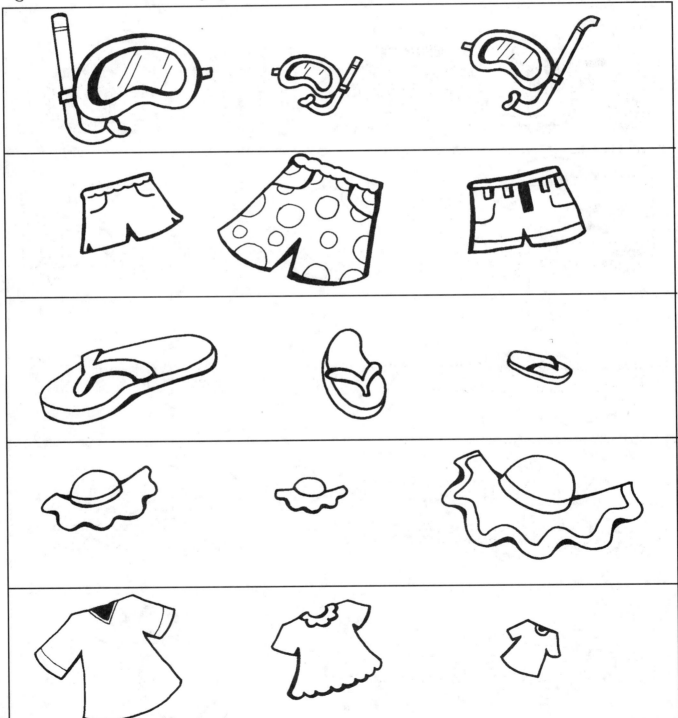

Longest

 Color the longest object in each row.

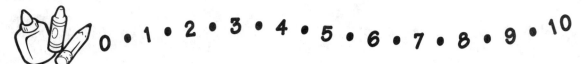

Shortest

Color the shortest object in each row.

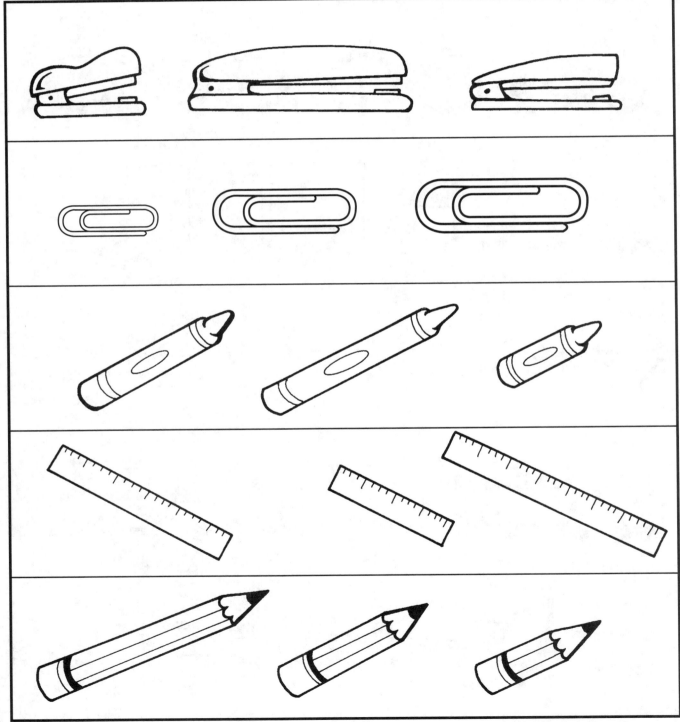

0 • 1 • 2 • 3 • 4 • 5 • 6 • 7 • 8 • 9 • 10

Buzzing Around

 Circle the bees' paths that are the same in each row.

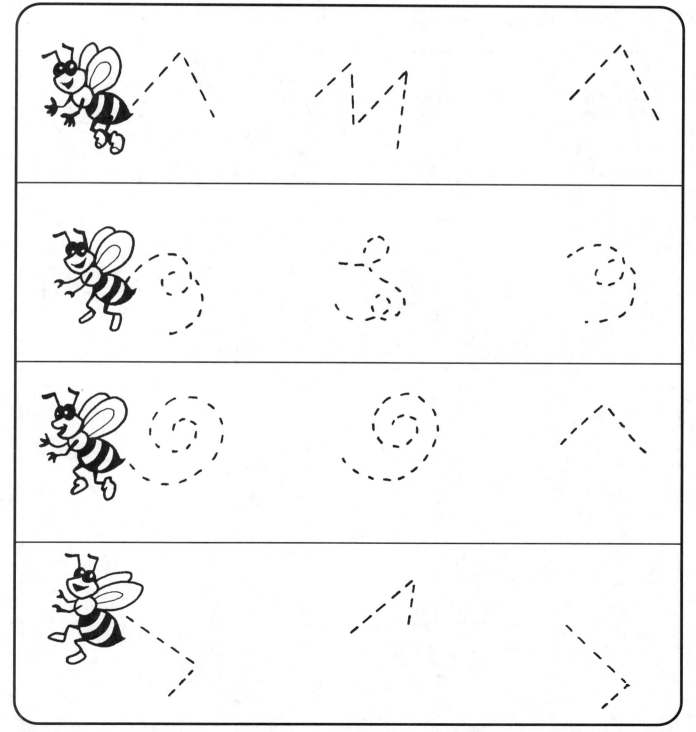

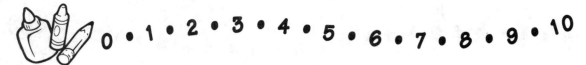

Beautiful Butterflies

 Cross out the butterfly that is different in each row.

 Color the matching butterflies in each row the same color.

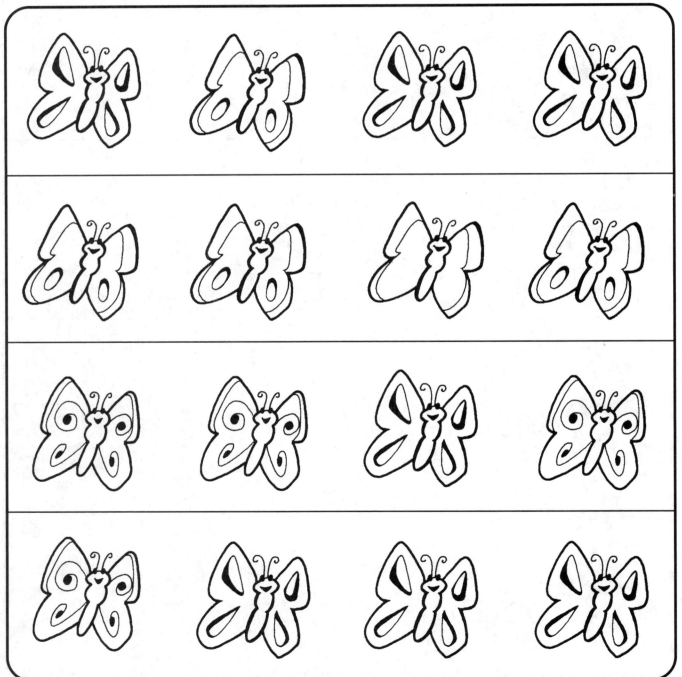

0 • 1 • 2 • 3 • 4 • 5 • 6 • 7 • 8 • 9 • 10

Hide and Seek

 Find and color each fish in the picture.

Count the fish and write the number below.

I found ☐ fish in all.

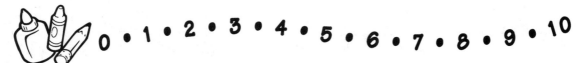

0 • 1 • 2 • 3 • 4 • 5 • 6 • 7 • 8 • 9 • 10

Where's My Bone?

Find and color the puppy's missing bones.

Count the bones and write the number below.

I found ☐ dog bones.

0 • 1 • 2 • 3 • 4 • 5 • 6 • 7 • 8 • 9 • 10

Bow Ties

 Draw a line to the bow ties that match.

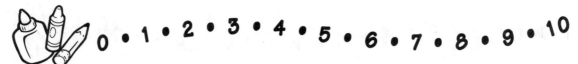

Going to the Zoo

 Practice writing the number <u>0</u> and the word <u>zero</u> on the lines below.

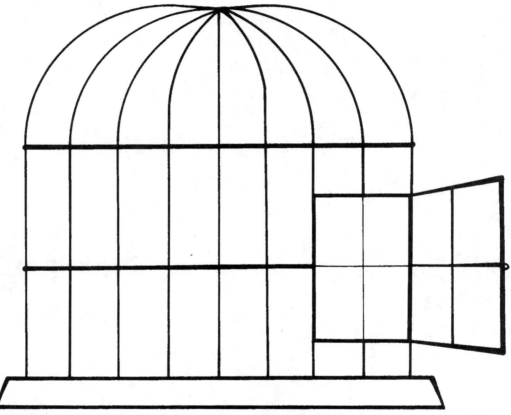

How many birds are in the cage?

0

zero

0 • 1 • 2 • 3 • 4 • 5 • 6 • 7 • 8 • 9 • 10

Going to the Zoo

 Practice writing the number 1 and the word <u>one</u> on the lines below.

| one

one

Going to the Zoo

 Practice writing the number <u>2</u> and the word <u>two</u> on the lines below.

2

2 two

two

0 • 1 • 2 • 3 • 4 • 5 • 6 • 7 • 8 • 9 • 10

Going to the Zoo

 Practice writing the number <u>3</u> and the word <u>three</u> on the lines below.

3

3 three

three

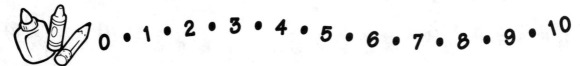

0 • 1 • 2 • 3 • 4 • 5 • 6 • 7 • 8 • 9 • 10

Going to the Zoo

 Practice writing the number 4 and the word <u>four</u> on the lines below.

4

4 four

four

0 • 1 • 2 • 3 • 4 • 5 • 6 • 7 • 8 • 9 • 10

Going to the Zoo

 Practice writing the number <u>5</u> and the word <u>five</u> on the lines below.

5

5 five

five

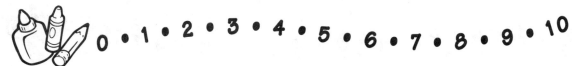

Going to the Zoo

 Practice writing the number <u>6</u> and the word <u>six</u> on the lines below.

6

6 six

six

0 • 1 • 2 • 3 • 4 • 5 • 6 • 7 • 8 • 9 • 10

Going to the Zoo

 Practice writing the number _7_ and the word <u>seven</u> on the lines below.

7

7 seven

seven

Numbers

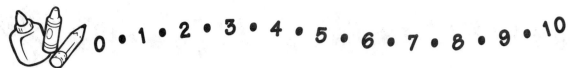

Going to the Zoo

 Practice writing the number <u>8</u> and the word <u>eight</u> on the lines below.

8

8 eight

eight

0 • 1 • 2 • 3 • 4 • 5 • 6 • 7 • 8 • 9 • 10

Going to the Zoo

Practice writing the number **9** and the word <u>nine</u> on the lines below.

9

9 nine

nine

0 • 1 • 2 • 3 • 4 • 5 • 6 • 7 • 8 • 9 • 10

Going to the Zoo

Practice writing the number <u>10</u> and the word <u>ten</u> on the lines below.

10

10 ten

ten

Color by Number

Color all the 0's blue.

Color all the 1's red.

Color by Number

Color all the 2's pink.

Color all the 3's purple.

Color by Number

 Color all the 4's brown.

Color all the 5's green.

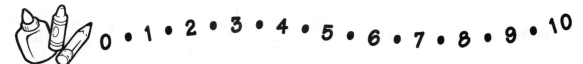

0 • 1 • 2 • 3 • 4 • 5 • 6 • 7 • 8 • 9 • 10

Color by Number

Color all the 6's blue.

Color all the 7's yellow.

0 • 1 • 2 • 3 • 4 • 5 • 6 • 7 • 8 • 9 • 10

Color by Number

 Color all the 8's orange.

Color all the 9's red.

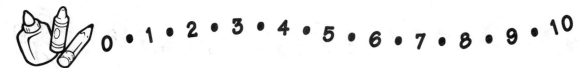

0 • 1 • 2 • 3 • 4 • 5 • 6 • 7 • 8 • 9 • 10

School Stop

Connect the dots from 1 – 10 to find out how the children get to school.

Color the bus yellow.

0 • 1 • 2 • 3 • 4 • 5 • 6 • 7 • 8 • 9 • 10

Abracadabra!

Connect the dots from 1–10 to see where the magician has hidden the rabbit.
Color your picture.

Let's Go!

Trace the numbers 1–5 in the first box of each row.

Color the correct number of cars in each row.

1	
2	
3	
4	
5	

0 • 1 • 2 • 3 • 4 • 5 • 6 • 7 • 8 • 9 • 10

Blast Off!

Trace the numbers 6–10 in the first box of each row.

Circle the correct number of rockets in each row.

6	🚀 🚀 🚀 🚀 🚀 🚀 🚀 🚀
7	🚀 🚀 🚀 🚀 🚀 🚀 🚀 🚀
8	🚀 🚀 🚀 🚀 🚀 🚀 🚀 🚀
9	🚀 🚀 🚀 🚀 🚀 🚀 🚀 🚀
10	🚀 🚀 🚀 🚀 🚀 🚀 🚀 🚀

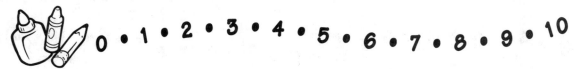

Bunches of Numbers

 Draw a line from the number to the matching set. Begin at the dot.

1 •

3 •

5 •

2 •

4 •

0 • 1 • 2 • 3 • 4 • 5 • 6 • 7 • 8 • 9 • 10

Bunches of Numbers

 Draw a line from the number to the matching set. Begin at the dot.

8•

10•

7•

9•

6•

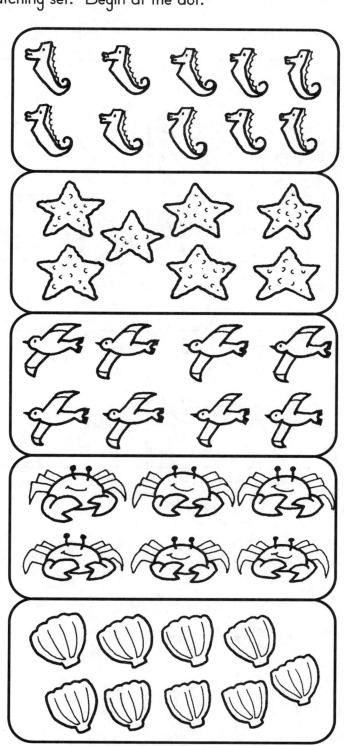

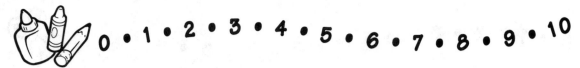

Fun in the Sun

 Read the number. Trace over the number in each box.

 Draw that amount of the object pictured in each box.

1 ☀	
2 🐾	
3 🏐	
4 🐚	
5 🪣	

    36

Fun in the Snow

 Read the number. Trace over the number in each box.

Draw that amount of the object pictured in each box.

6	
7	
8	
9	
10	

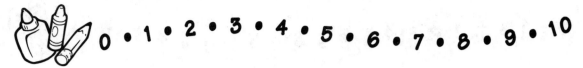

Fun at School

 Read the number.

Draw that amount of the object pictured in each box.

1	2
3	4
5	6
7	8
9	10

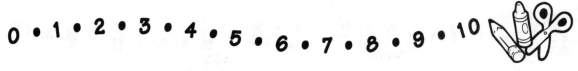

Birthday Fun

 Draw candles on the cake. Use the number to tell how many to draw.

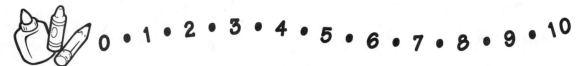

Cookie Count

 Draw cookies in the jars. Use the number to tell how many to draw.

0 • 1 • 2 • 3 • 4 • 5 • 6 • 7 • 8 • 9 • 10

It's Raining

 Draw raindrops from the clouds. Use the number to tell you how many to draw.

q

8

7

10

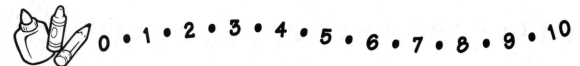

Bugs

 Count the bugs' spots in each box and circle the correct number.

1 3 2	5 3 4
6 8 7	8 10 9
6 5 4	7 8 9
7 5 6	4 3 2

0 • 1 • 2 • 3 • 4 • 5 • 6 • 7 • 8 • 9 • 10

Set Them Up 3 - 6

 Cut out the numbers below.

Glue the numbers next to the matching set.

	🎳 🎳 🎳 🎳
	🎳 🎳 🎳 🎳 🎳 🎳
	🎳 🎳 🎳
	🎳 🎳 🎳 🎳 🎳

- -

| 3 | 4 | 5 | 6 |

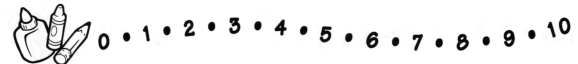

Set Them Up 7 - 10

✂ Cut out the numbers below.

🖍 Glue them next to the matching set.

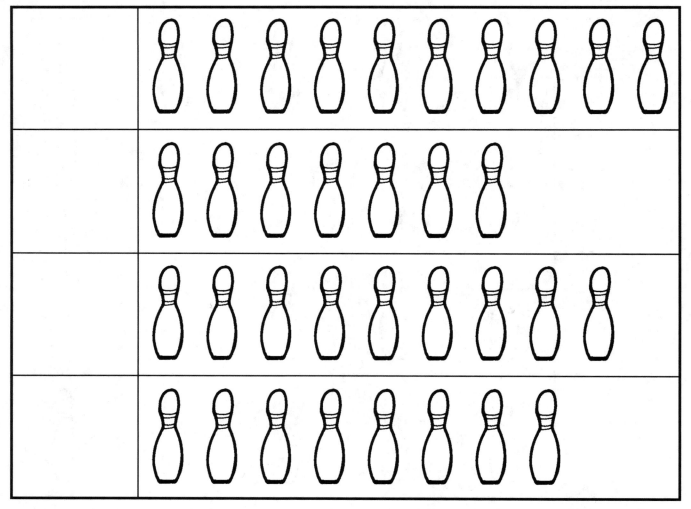

7   8   9   10

Closet Count 1-5

 Write the number of each object in the boxes below.

How many 👡 ? [ ]   How many empty 🪝 ? [ ]

How many 👔 ? [ ]   How many 👗 ? [ ]

How many 👒 ? [ ]

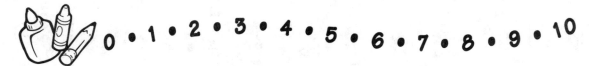

How Does Your Garden Grow?
6 - 10

 Write the number of each object in the boxes below.

How many ? ☐   How many ? ☐

How many ? ☐   How many ? ☐

How many ? ☐

0 • 1 • 2 • 3 • 4 • 5 • 6 • 7 • 8 • 9 • 10

Bubble Gum, Bubble Gum

 Write the number of bubble gum pieces in the box next to each machine.

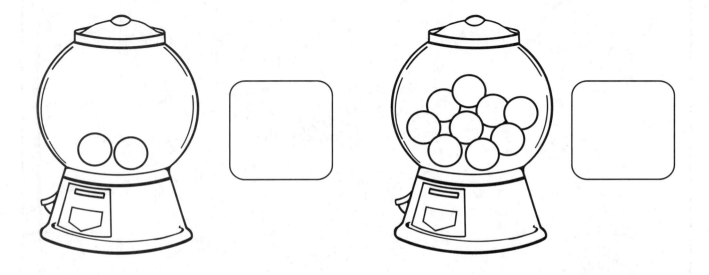

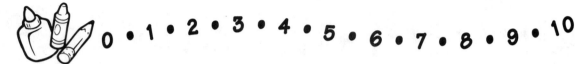

Gumdrop Count

 Write the number of gumdrops pieces in the box next to each bowl.

0 • 1 • 2 • 3 • 4 • 5 • 6 • 7 • 8 • 9 • 10

Hey Diddle, Diddle

 Circle the object at the end of the row that finishes the pattern.

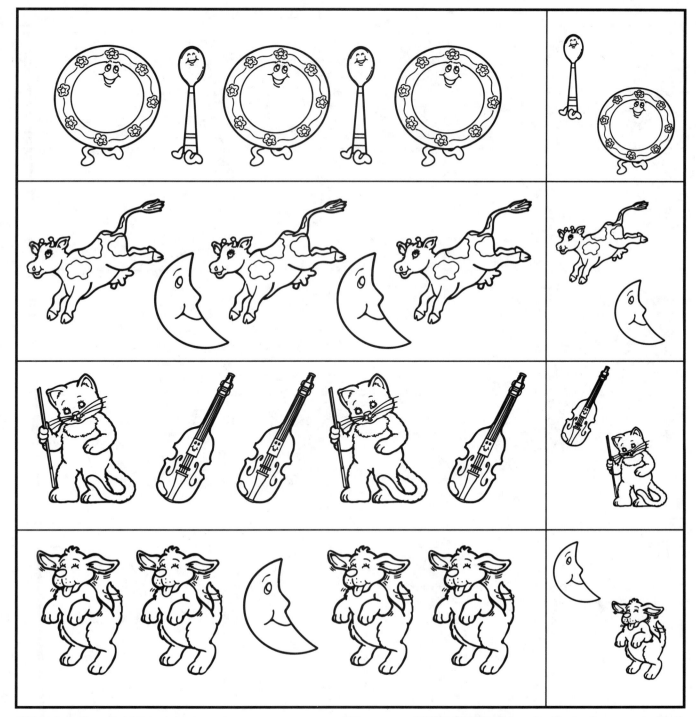

Flying High

Cut out the pictures below.

Glue them in the box at the end of each row to finish the pattern.

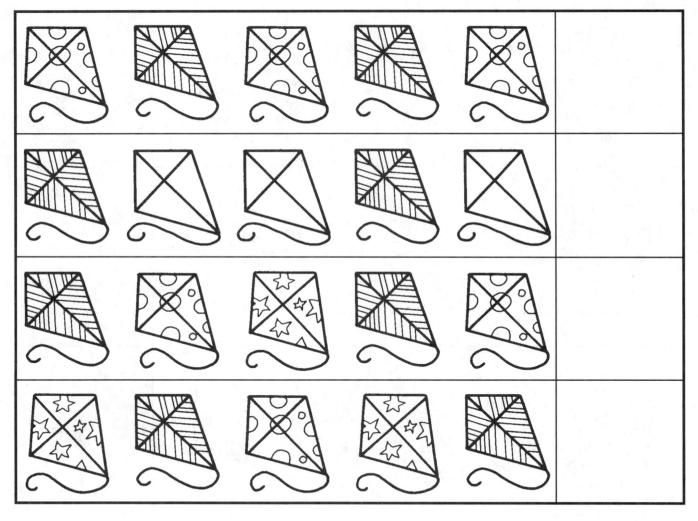

What Comes Next?

 Finish the patterns in each row.

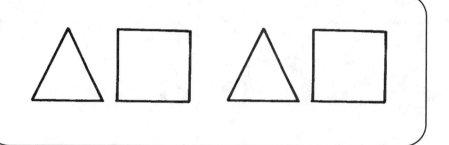

1 2 3 1 2 3 1 2

Number Patterning

 Cut out the numbers below.

Glue them in the box at the end of each row to finish the pattern.

5 6 5 6 5 6 5 6	
8 7 7 8 7 7 8 7	
6 7 8 6 7 8 6 7	
5 7 6 5 7 6 5 7	

5	6	7	8

Expressions

 Draw an expression on the faces in the boxes on the right to finish the patterns.

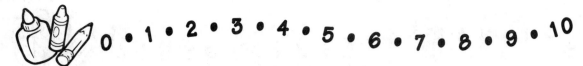 0 • 1 • 2 • 3 • 4 • 5 • 6 • 7 • 8 • 9 • 10

Monkey Business

 Cut out the banana and monkey cards below. Create different patterns with them.

0 • 1 • 2 • 3 • 4 • 5 • 6 • 7 • 8 • 9 • 10

What Comes First?

 Color the first heart red.

 Color the third heart yellow.

 Color the second heart blue.

 Color the third child's shirt green.

 Color the second child's shirt orange.

 Color the first child's shirt purple.

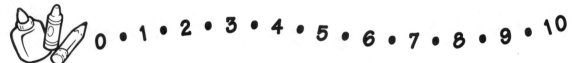

In the Middle

 Draw a smile on the last face.

 Draw a frown on the middle face.

 Draw a straight line for the mouth on the first face.

 Draw a hat on the last snowman.

 Draw a scarf on the first snowman.

 Draw a carrot nose on the middle snowman.

Helping Hands

 Cut along the dashed lines and arrange the pictures in the order given.

 Glue the police officer in the 1st box.   Glue the firefighter in the 2nd box.

 Glue the teacher in the 3rd box.   Glue the mail carrier in the 4th box.

1st	2nd	3rd	4th

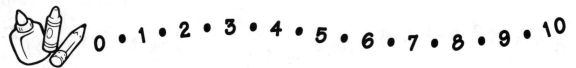

Button Up

✂ Cut out and sort the buttons below.

🖌 Glue them on the coats with the same shape button.

🖍 Circle the coat that has the most buttons.

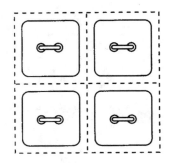

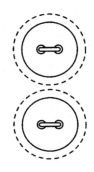

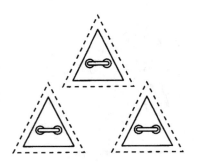

0 • 1 • 2 • 3 • 4 • 5 • 6 • 7 • 8 • 9 • 10

Eggs-actly

 Cut out and sort the eggs below.

 Glue them according to size in the nests.

 Circle the nest that has the largest eggs.

- -

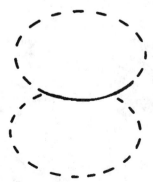

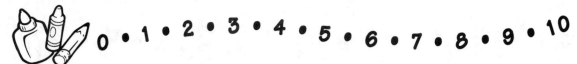

0 • 1 • 2 • 3 • 4 • 5 • 6 • 7 • 8 • 9 • 10

Marble Fun

✂ Cut out and sort the marbles below.

🍶 Glue them according to design in the marble bags.

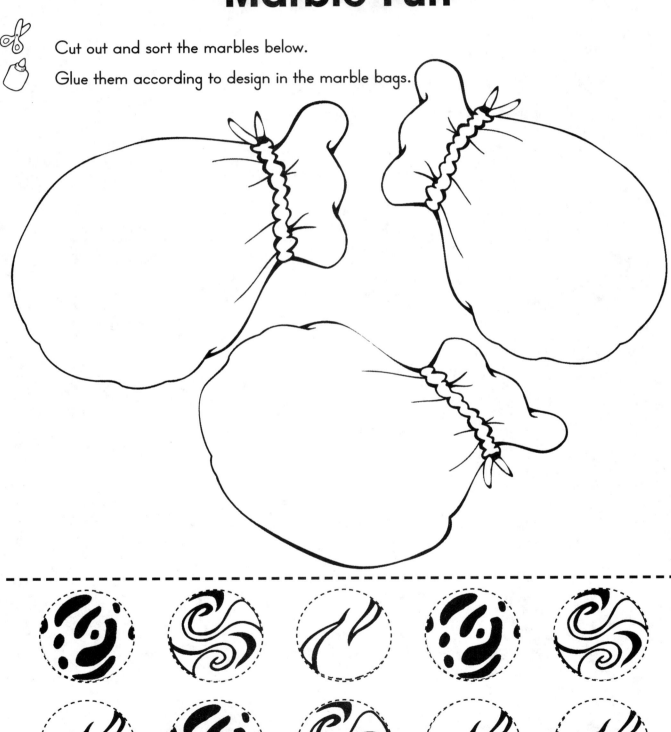

0 • 1 • 2 • 3 • 4 • 5 • 6 • 7 • 8 • 9 • 10

Who's Been Eating My Porridge?

 Color the bears' bowls.

Cut out the bears' bowls.

Glue them in order from smallest to largest.

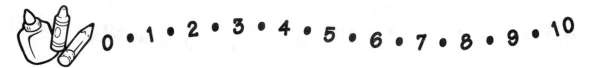

Who's Been Sitting in My Chair?

 Cut out the bears and their chairs.

 Glue them in order from largest to smallest.

0 • 1 • 2 • 3 • 4 • 5 • 6 • 7 • 8 • 9 • 10

Who's Been Sleeping in my Bed?

 Cut out the bears' beds and their pillows.

Glue them in order from smallest to largest.

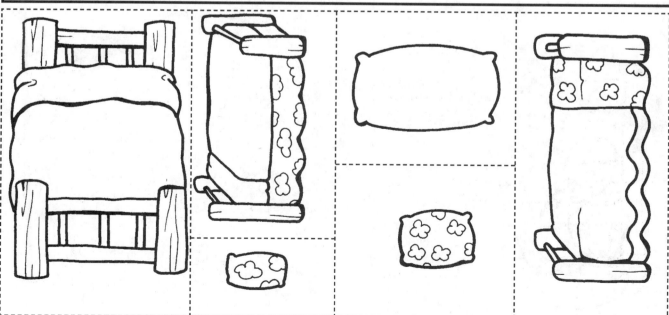

Circles

 Trace the gray circles.

Practice making your own circles by adding more balloons.

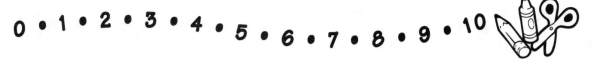

0 • 1 • 2 • 3 • 4 • 5 • 6 • 7 • 8 • 9 • 10

Squares

 Trace the squares.

 Practice making your own squares by adding more windows.

Triangles

 Trace the triangles.

 Practice making your own triangles by adding more sails.

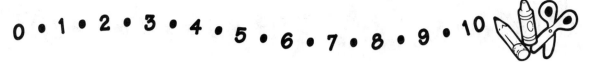

Rectangles

 Trace the rectangles.

Practice making your own rectangles by making more train cars.

Which Match?

✂️ Cut out each object.

🧴 Glue each object to the matching shape.

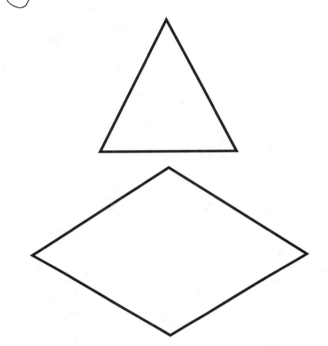

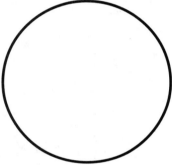

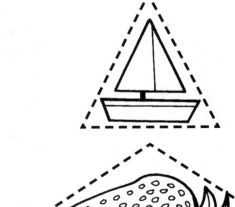

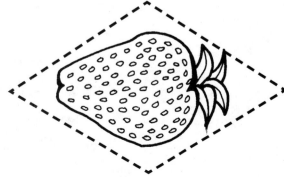

0 • 1 • 2 • 3 • 4 • 5 • 6 • 7 • 8 • 9 • 10

Shape Match

 Color the object that matches the shape in each row. Name the shape.

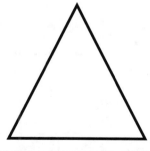 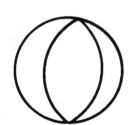 

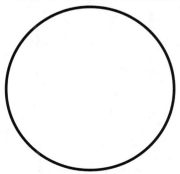  

       #3686 Skill Builders for Young Learners: Math

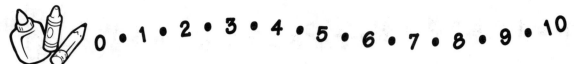

Color by Shape

 Color the triangles blue.

Color the rectangles red.

Color the squares orange.

Color the circles green.

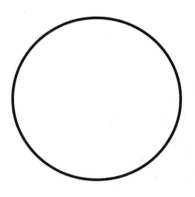  

 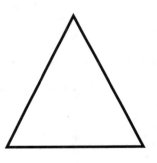 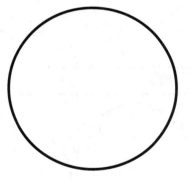 

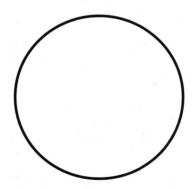  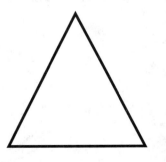 

0 • 1 • 2 • 3 • 4 • 5 • 6 • 7 • 8 • 9 • 10

Shape Word Trace

 Trace the name under each shape. Color each shape a different color.

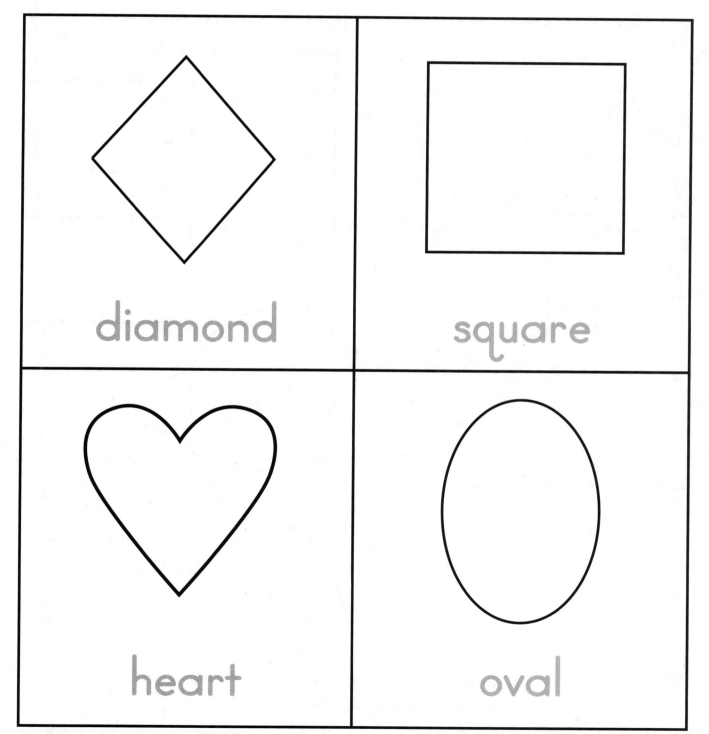

diamond

square

heart

oval

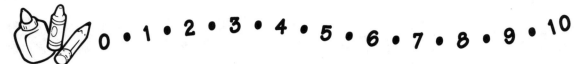

Shape Word Trace

Trace the name under each shape. Color each shape a different color.

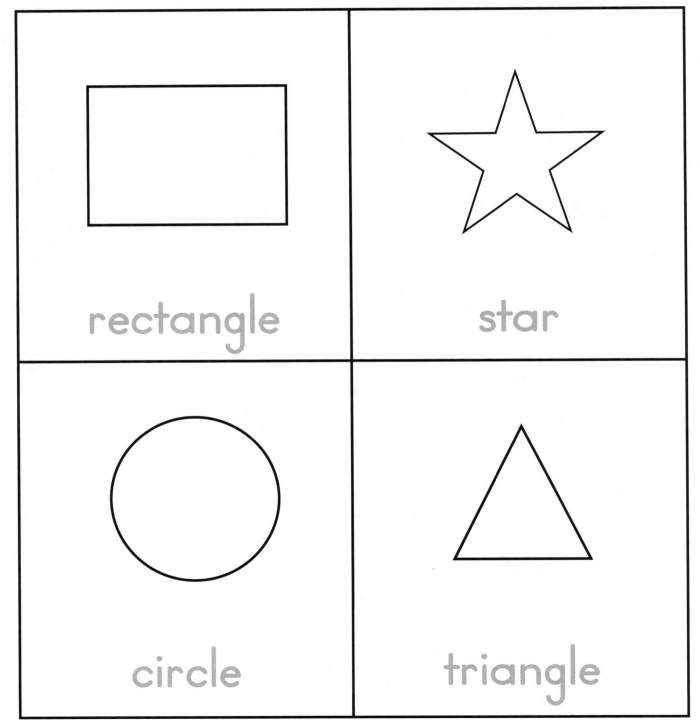

rectangle

star

circle

triangle

0 • 1 • 2 • 3 • 4 • 5 • 6 • 7 • 8 • 9 • 10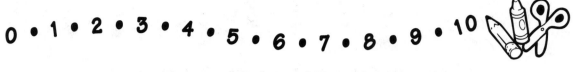

Shape Match

 Draw a line to match each shape to its name.

   rectangle

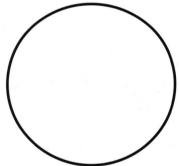   star

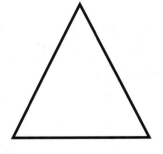   circle

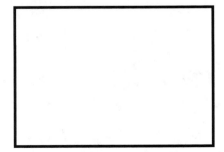   triangle

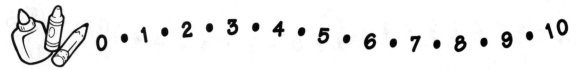

Shape Match

 Draw a line to match each shape to its name.

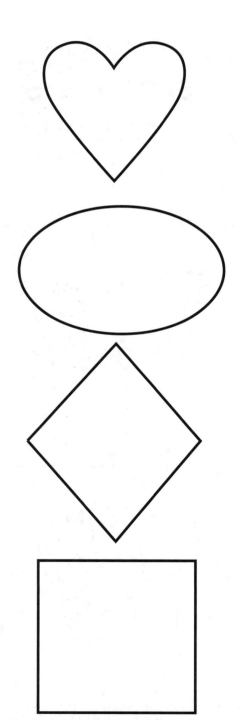

diamond

square

heart

oval

0 • 1 • 2 • 3 • 4 • 5 • 6 • 7 • 8 • 9 • 10

Special Delivery

 Color the mailbox in each row that has more mail.

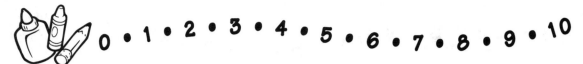

Flower Power

 Color the vase in each row that has fewer flowers.

76

0 • 1 • 2 • 3 • 4 • 5 • 6 • 7 • 8 • 9 • 10

Down on the Farm

 In each row, circle the set of objects that has more.

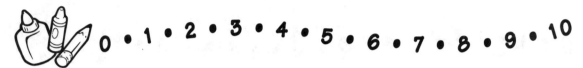

Old MacDonald's Pals

 Circle the set of each animal in the row that has less.

0 • 1 • 2 • 3 • 4 • 5 • 6 • 7 • 8 • 9 • 10

Party Time

Draw a line from one set of objects to the set with the same number.

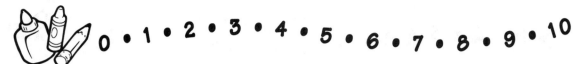

This Little Piggy

Fill in the missing numbers by counting from 1—9.

0 • 1 • 2 • 3 • 4 • 5 • 6 • 7 • 8 • 9 • 10

Ducks in a Row

 Fill in the missing numbers in each row.

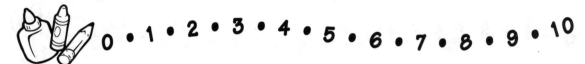

Crayon Count

✂ Cut out the crayons below.

Glue them in order from 1–5.

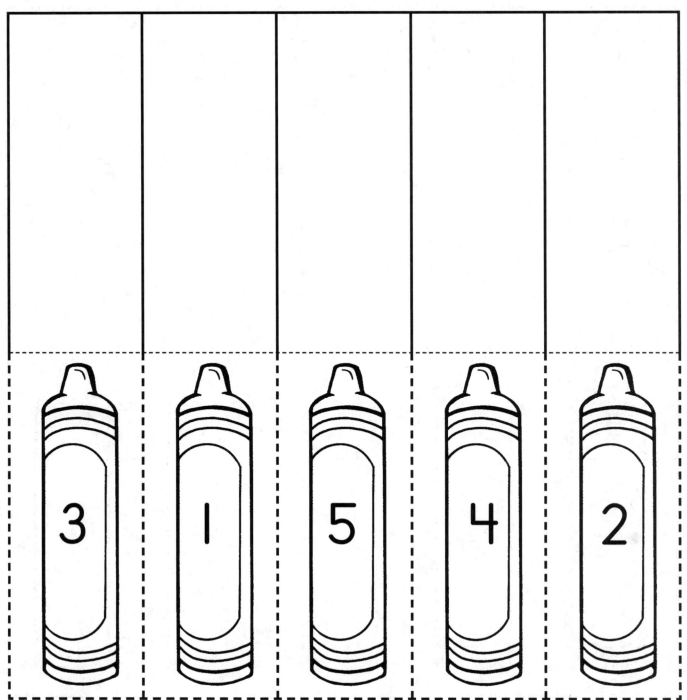

0 • 1 • 2 • 3 • 4 • 5 • 6 • 7 • 8 • 9 • 10

Crayon Count

 Cut out the crayons below.

 Glue them in order from 6–10.

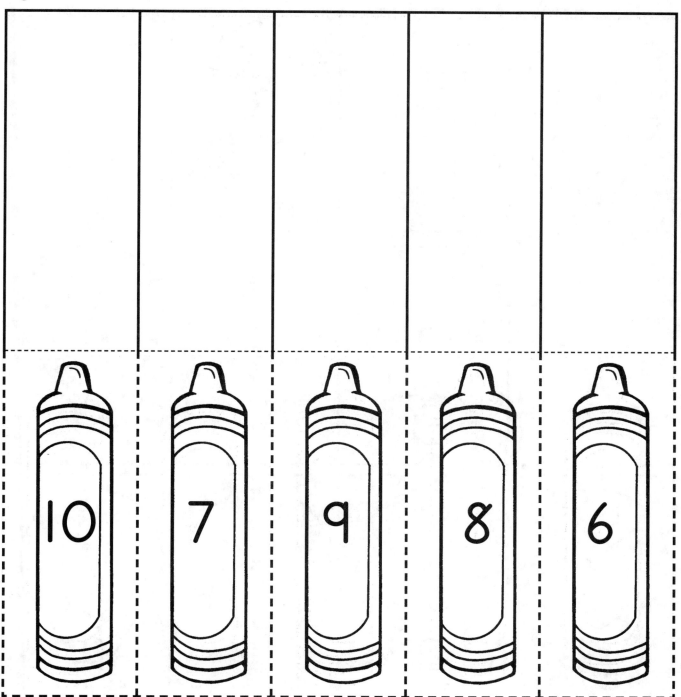

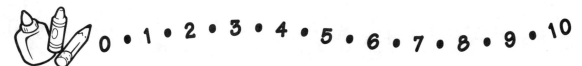

0 • 1 • 2 • 3 • 4 • 5 • 6 • 7 • 8 • 9 • 10

Up, Up and Away

✂ Cut out the balloons below.

🖊 Glue them in order from 1–8.

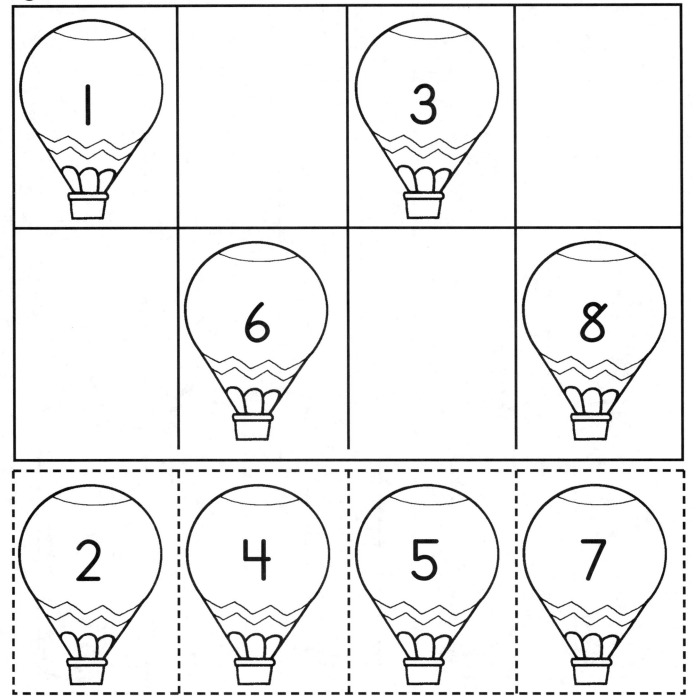

0 • 1 • 2 • 3 • 4 • 5 • 6 • 7 • 8 • 9 • 10

Wiggle Worms

 Fill in the missing numbers in each row.

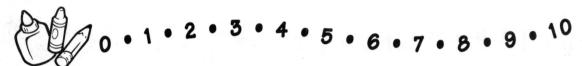

0 • 1 • 2 • 3 • 4 • 5 • 6 • 7 • 8 • 9 • 10

Caterpillar Crawl

✂ Cut out the circles at the bottom of the page.

🧴 Glue the circles in the correct order.

0 • 1 • 2 • 3 • 4 • 5 • 6 • 7 • 8 • 9 • 10

All Aboard!

Fill in the missing numbers on the train.

0 • 1 • 2 • 3 • 4 • 5 • 6 • 7 • 8 • 9 • 10

Buried Treasure

Draw a line to match the number to the word.

1
0
3
2
4
5

zero
three
four
one
five
two

0 • 1 • 2 • 3 • 4 • 5 • 6 • 7 • 8 • 9 • 10

Jungle Adventure

 Draw a line to match the number to the word.

7	ten
6	six
9	seven
10	eight
8	nine

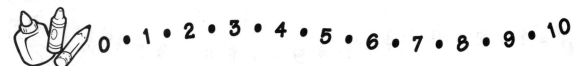

Crown Jewels

Draw a line from the number set to the number word.
(Hint: Count the jewels in each crown.)

- three

- one

- two

- four

- five

0 • 1 • 2 • 3 • 4 • 5 • 6 • 7 • 8 • 9 • 10

Wizard's Hat

 Count the stars in each wizard hat. Draw a line from the number word to the hat with the correct number of stars.

seven •

six •

eight •

ten •

nine •

Pet Addition

Count the animals in each row and add them together.

Write the total in the box at the end of the row.

🐱 + 🐱 =	
🐶 🐶 + 🐶 =	
🐦 🐦 + 🐦 🐦 =	
🐹 + 🐹 🐹 =	
🐢 🐢 🐢 + 🐢 =	

0 • 1 • 2 • 3 • 4 • 5 • 6 • 7 • 8 • 9 • 10

Ball Game!

 Count the objects in each row and add them together.

Write the total in the box at the end of the row.

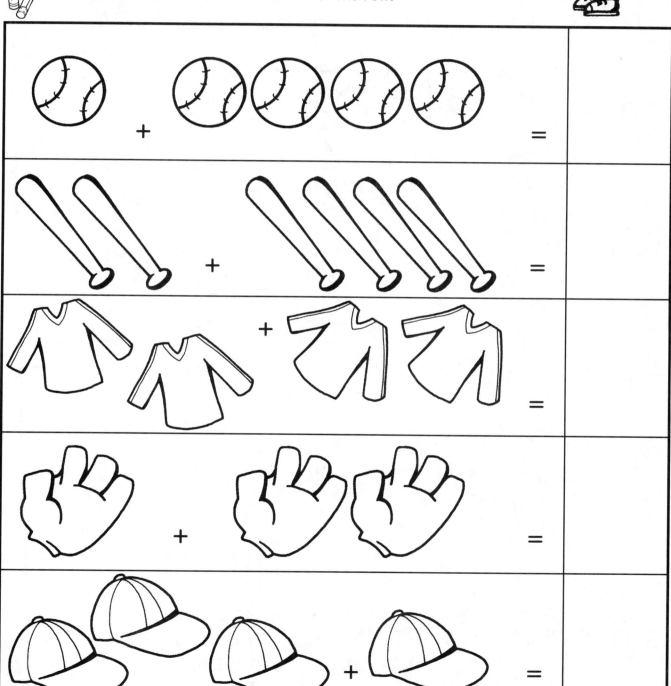

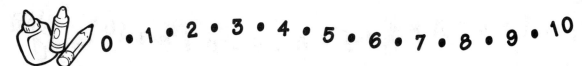

Go Nuts!

 Count the squirrel's nuts in each row and add them together.

Write the total in the box at the end of the row.

🌰 + 🌰 🌰 🌰 🌰 =	
🌰 🌰 + 🌰 🌰 🌰 =	
🌰 🌰 🌰 + 🌰 🌰 🌰 =	
🌰 🌰 + 🌰 🌰 =	
🌰 🌰 🌰 + 🌰 🌰 🌰 🌰 =	

0 • 1 • 2 • 3 • 4 • 5 • 6 • 7 • 8 • 9 • 10

Picnic Lunch

 Add the items in each row and write the total in the box.

🍉 + 🍉 🍉 =	
cans + cans =	
hot dogs + hot dogs =	
cups + cups =	
corn + corn =	

Gone Fishing

Count the fish in each box and add them together.

Write the total in the box at the end of the row.

96 ©Teacher Created Materials, Inc.